60 Minute
Public Speaking

STEWART LANCASTER

ISBN: 1499376839
ISBN-13: 978-1499376838

CONTENTS

PREFACE

My Public Speaking journey…

In the early 2000's I was the Head of Operations for a large financial brokerage. I had been running a project to build our own in house training program to allow us to train new employees as financial advisers. I had appointed two senior members of the team to carefully design a gruelling week of intensive training which culminated in delegates sitting their regulatory exams at the end of the week.

It was a Friday morning and finally all of our

hard work and preparation was about to pay off. I had been monitoring the progress of this project by way of weekly update meetings and was excited to welcome twenty new recruits to our inaugural training course the following Monday.

Just after 9:00 am my senior trainer walked into my office and asked if I had a few minutes to discuss the course. I invited him to take a seat and couldn't help but notice that he wasn't quite looking himself, he looked like he had seen a ghost.

There was a pause that became a lengthy silence which was eventually followed by a confession. He had been a little optimistic in his weekly project updates and that in fact he had not even created the course introduction. At this point we had nothing more than a brief agenda.

It turned out that he had a crippling fear of public speaking, so extreme that he could barely commit pen to paper. Initially I thought about cancelling the course, but quickly realised that 20 people were relying on me and my team.

Immediately I cleared my diary for the day and told my team that we had 'an issue' that I had to resolve personally, and to that effect I would be leaving the office to work on the course material all weekend.

How could this have happened? How did this issue not come to light in our weekly update meetings? How was I going to create a weeks' worth of training material in two and a half days? These were all of the questions that raced through my head as I left the office; then it dawned on me, I had to speak to a room full of 20 strangers for an entire week. This was public speaking at its extreme.

Monday morning came around in what seemed like a flash and my mind was racing, I was trying to find an excuse as to why I couldn't go into work that day. I couldn't call in sick as everyone would know that I was terrified and under prepared. The answer came out of the blue, a car crash! Just a little crash so I couldn't come into the office, nothing too serious but just enough to avoid this public speaking experience.

Thankfully my rational mind took over and I

didn't crash my car. I turned up early, loaded my presentation, practiced my introduction and waited for the delegates to arrive. By 9:30 there were twenty new faces staring back at me.

Despite feeling frozen with fear, I began my introduction and survived what felt like the longest ninety minutes of my career until we had our first planned break. Everyone had left the room to get refreshments but I knew they would be back within 15 minutes, this was the morning of the first day, how was I going to survive 5 days of this?

Before I knew it the room was full again and I continued with the course, all I had to do was survive another 90 minutes and we would break for lunch.

I delivered the second half of the morning's content and then dismissed the class for lunch. This time something had changed; I'm not sure when but at some point in the second half of the morning I had moved from a state of physical fear to enjoying the experience. I was confident, energised and actually looking forward to delivering the afternoon's material.

This continued for the rest of the week and I am happy to report that 17 out of the 20 students passed their exams on their first sitting, which was considerably higher than the 50% pass rate across the industry. The course was a success.

You may be able to relate in some part to my story, being asked to speak to a group of people and feeling under prepared. You may be able to relate to the fear. If this is such a feared topic, why would anyone want to improve or even master this skill? It is Human nature to move towards experiences that give us pleasure and move away from experiences that cause us pain, so picking up a book on public speaking appears to be counter intuitive to say the least, however, the fact remains that public speaking is an important skill and it is fundamental in many careers, particularly in management and leadership roles.

This book is designed to help you with three things:

1. Create a clear and concise speech,

2. Deliver a compelling speech, and

3. Reduce your levels of anxiety about public speaking

More specifically this book is designed to help you learn all of the above in less than 60 minutes. A bit of a challenging task perhaps, to learn a new way of thinking in less time than it takes to watch a movie, but one that I am sure, if you are reading this that you have the appetite, the determination and the will to complete this task.

In writing this book, I have had to use a number of cutting edge models to try and deeply implant everything you read in the next 60 minutes into your long term memory including connecting left brain (reading, writing, listening, logic and sequence) and right brain (images, colour, music, creativity and intuition), a phenomenon known as the "primary" and "recency" effect and finally a number of memory consolidation techniques.

The brain has a four step process which is always followed in the formation of every new memory:

Encoding:	This is the process of reading or learning the new material
Consolidation:	This is where the newly learnt information is repeated, often in different forms to the point where you feel you have 'memorised' the information (short term memory only)
Storage:	This is where the information is moved into your long term memory
Retrieval:	The ability to recall the information at will

The techniques described above focus predominantly in the memory consolidation stage, which increases the likelihood of forming long term memories.

To help aid this process and ensure your

success you may wish to do the following:

Avoid distraction: Don't get me wrong, you WILL lose focus and you WILL be distracted during the course of this book, this is simply human nature and more importantly the nature of our brains. You can minimise these effects by reading somewhere you will not be too distracted that is not too noisy to concentrate.

Repetition: Try to repeat the models and methods you learn in this book, say them out loud, write and re-write them until you are able to recall them without looking at the text. Repeating this exercise within the next 24 and 48 hours will help in transferring these memories into your long term memory (memory encoding, consolidation and storage)

Chunking: Your brain has the ability to focus for finite periods and tends to recall more at the beginning and the end of a sequence. Beyond this, memory recall is diminished. Use this inherent feature to your advantage and try to break this book down into smaller, more memorable chunks, (as a rule of thumb to calculate your optimum focus period you should use your age plus or minus two minutes) creating multiple start/stop points. Take a 5 - 15 minute break between sections and review what you have read, draw diagrams or simply go for a walk. These are all ways of supporting the memory creation process.

Highlight: Use the highlighting feature in

your kindle to draw attention to specific parts of the text, this will help you recall key points and will further aid future repetition, if you have time use these highlighted sections to create cheat sheets that will allow you to anchor the method into your brain, highlight and underline to your heart's content but most of all, enjoy.

Listen to Music: You may think that this contradicts the previous advice to avoid distractions but the link between (certain types of) music and increased memory recall is well documented and widely accepted (often referred to as the 'Mozart Effect'). Quietly playing classical music in the background or through headphones can increase your ability to concentrate for longer periods.

Doodle: As you come across concepts in this book draw diagrams, create pictures and models to help you remember what you have learnt. Use pictures, colours, make them funny, obscure, fantastical, rude and personal to ensure that these are a powerful aid to recall.

As with all of these suggestions, try them, use whatever works for you, and file the rest for future use; this is all about building long terms memories to support your endeavours.

Throughout this book you will see references to the term 'speech' but this can essentially be replaced with the term 'meeting', 'presentation' or any other context as appropriate for your situation; whatever environment you need to present in the principles will remain the same.

CHAPTER 1: YOU NEED A PLAN

Public speaking is in essence the study and application of rhetoric; rhetoric is usually defined something like this:

"An art that aims to improve the capability of writers or speakers to inform, persuade, or motivate particular audiences in specific situations." (Source: Wikipedia)

I want to correct this myth:

Public speaking is not an art.

Public speaking is not a science.

Public speaking is a trade.

I want you to remember this analogy over the next 60 minutes.

As with any trade there are a series of tools and the key is to understand which tools to use and when and finally, how to use them correctly. When you begin to learn a trade, you learn the basic principles, such as hammering, sawing, measuring, joining etc., you learn in this way so you understand the basic principles and can apply them to any situation.

Building blocks of public speaking

Around 50 BC a Roman Rhetorician called Cicero identified 5 building blocks of public speaking. Public speaking as an art form was further developed over the course of 150 years and distilled by Quintilian in 95 AD in a detailed, 12 volume series of books, labelled the "Five Cannons of Rhetoric". These studies formed the foundation of the study of rhetoric well into the middle ages and have stood the test of time and to this day form the basis of many of the best known speeches in recent history.

5 Cannons of Rhetoric:

- Memory

- Arrangement

- Invention

- Delivery

- Style

These are essentially the 5 building blocks of the house that we are going to build together over the next 60 minutes

Memory:

Memory was historically linked to both committing a speech to memory as well as having a knowledge bank of useful stories, anecdotes and examples that you can use in your speech. In our context memory relates to remembering your speech's arrangement. *The process of learning and memorizing your speech so you can deliver it without the use of notes.*

Arrangement:

Arrangement relates to the structure and

the order of the speech. It is the logical flow of information designed to support your ideas and is linked to the building block of invention. *The process of arranging and organizing your arguments for maximum impact.*

Invention:

Invention is at its core the ability to find something to say, it is the process of creating your argument, your assertions and your support which could include cause and effect, comparison or relational arguments. Invention can simply be summarised as what a speaker would say rather than how this might be said. *The process of developing and refining your arguments.*

Delivery:

Delivery relates to how something is said, rather than what is said. Essentially pitch, tone, pace, body language and gestures. *The process of practicing how you deliver your speech using gestures, pronunciation, and tone of voice.*

Style:

Style relates to the words and the message they convey. The style building block ensures that the language conveys powerful picture messages into the mind of the audience that they can easily understand and remember. *The process of determining how you present your arguments using figures of speech and other rhetorical techniques.*

We are going to further develop these building blocks in the next few chapters. Chapter 3: Crafting your speech will walk you through the first three building blocks and give you the tools to create powerful content, later, Chapter 4: Doing it in style will take you through the final two building blocks and show you how to deliver your speech with presence and natural confidence.

The key to effortless public speaking

I am now going to share with you the secret the effortless public speaking…

Preparation.

Ironically yes, the key to effortless public speaking is effort, however it is about ensuring that you have put the required effort in before you are called upon to speak. That you have invested in yourself and have developed the skills you will learn in the coming chapters; but also invested time and energy creating a compelling presentation ahead of time, not simply thinking on your feet and bluffing your way through the few minutes of the presentation.

Can you imagine a tradesman (let's say a plasterer) plastering his first wall; he completes the task, stands back to admire his work, sees an imperfection and immediately puts his tools away, vowing to never plaster again!

Typically people forego the preparation stage of effective public speaking and rely on their speaking abilities 'on the day' to carry them through the performance' those that do prepare will often rehearse the entire speech from start to finish as many as three times. If this seems like a lot of unnecessary work to you then you will be surprised to hear that professional public speakers will usually practice entire presentations a minimum of thirty times, varying the introduction or conclusion, trying different stories to illustrate key points, just to be able to deliver a credible performance once.

Preparation is a force that you need to act on in order for it to have an effect, you need to be proactive and without it nothing happens. It is rumoured that English Prime Minister Winston Churchill spent one hour preparing for every one minute of his speech.

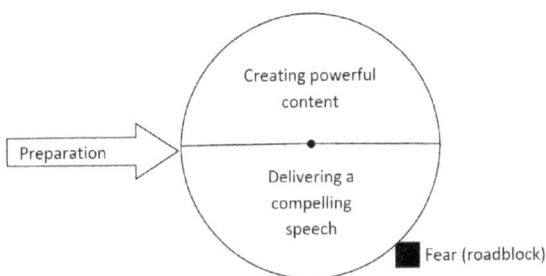

However if you are overwhelmed by the fear of public speaking then this is like a roadblock in the way of your success and even and small amount of fear can greatly reduce your public speaking abilities meaning you will need to apply far more force to overcome your fear.

In the next chapter we are going to look at reducing the fear of public speaking.

Summary:

Public speaking is an important and worthwhile skill that can be learnt in less than 60 minutes. Fact. There are few born public speakers and at its most basic, as a skill it is inextricably linked to career success.

Managers at all levels are expected to be able to communicate clearly and concisely. Put simply, to lead effectively you must be able to communicate direction and goals effectively; this is even more important as you progress to the top of an organisation and becomes an expectation at board level.

There are few 'born' public speakers; importantly this means that there are thousands of 'polished' public speakers. If thousands of others have learned to speak effectively in public then you can too. With a few simple tools you will be able to master the art of creating compelling content and delivering a powerful speech.

Through the next few chapters you will learn more about this important and worthwhile skill as well as a simple framework to help you remember this for years to come. I would like to wish you the very best on your public speaking journey.

Remember:

There are two key points to remember in this chapter, the building blocks of public speaking and the foundation of any good speech:

1. Building blocks of public speaking:

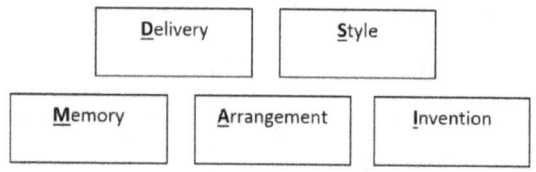

The Mnemonic to help you remember the five building block is the word "MAIDS"

2. The foundation of any good speech is:

Preparation

To really increase your chances of successful recall you should draw out these diagrams, adding your own notes, and mnemonics as you go until you have committed this to memory, repeat this process in one day and then again in one week to push this into your long term memory.

CHAPTER 2: REDUCING THE FEAR OF PUBLIC SPEAKING

Scenario:

You have been asked to attend a one day training course with a group of individuals that you have never met before. The desks are arranged in a 'U' shape and you decide to sit in an empty chair to the far left of the room next to a flip chart to give you the best view, you take out a brand new notepad and pen from your bag and you begin to feel a sense of nostalgia, almost like the first day of school, as you place them on your desk.

As more and more people arrive before the training course begins you start to make polite conversation with the rest of the class; this continues until the trainer walks stands up and begins to introduce herself along with the agenda for the day. At this point you feel completely calm, relaxed and even looking forward to what you are going to learn.

Once the housekeeping is out of the way, and everyone is aware of the location of the fire exits and has turned their mobile phones off, the trainer announces that in a moment she is going to ask you all to stand up one at a time and briefly introduce yourself, followed by a few brief sentences about your role and what you hope to get out of the course.

Immediately you are overcome with a sense of panic. Your mind races as you desperately try to think of something remotely intelligent to say.

Despite having been in the same role for the last two years you cannot seem to find a single interesting thing to say about your job; in fact at this point you can't even seem to articulate what your job is!

Before you can gather your thoughts the trainer announces that she is going to work around the classroom from her right; looks directly at you and asks you to stand.

You take a deep breath and in an attempt

to make sure this horrible experience is over you pour out a series of words at a hundred miles an hour. A minute later the trainer thanks you and you sit back down, red faced and flustered as you try to recall what you actually said. You try to look interested as you pretend to listen to each member of the course as they seem to naturally stand up and address the course almost effortlessly all the while you are asking yourself "why can't I just do that".

How is it that in less than a minute you went from being completely relaxed to the point of enjoying a polite conversation with your fellow students, to being in an uncontrollable state of panic whilst telling the same individuals very basic information about yourself?

How to overcome the fear of public speaking

Many people have a profound fear of public speaking, this is an almost universal fear and is perfectly natural. Being natural does not make it helpful and the fear of public speaking can be crippling to both your confidence and your career.

I want you to get a fresh sheet of paper and write down the following question:

"Why am I scared of public speaking?"

Now, spend a few moments thinking about this question and when you have an answer I want you to write your answer directly below the question on the same piece of paper. There are a number of reasons why people fear public speaking and your answer may look something like the following:

- I am scared of not knowing what to say or of running out of things to say

- I am scared of not being able to fill the time allocated

- I am scared of not being able to respond to a difficult question

- I am scared of looking 'stupid'

Many of these fears are what I refer to as 'subordinate fears' and are specifically related to content and delivery, thankfully both of these are skills that are easily learnt and you will come across simple yet powerful models to craft a compelling speech along with the skills of delivering an effective speech later in this book.

I refer to them as subordinate fears as they are essentially the mind's way of rationalising and internalising the 'dangers' of public speaking. Your subconscious will tell you that "you will run out of things to say" or "you will look like an idiot in front of your boss" or anything else that will be convincing enough to ensure that you never stand up and speak ever again. The true source of public speaking fear actually lies elsewhere.

Have you ever seen a young child stand up in front of a group of strangers and introduce them self? Do they spend hours preparing? Do they panic? Or do they simply stand and say whatever comes naturally to them in an entirely confident way?

How is it possible that something as natural as speaking, a skill that incidentally you mastered before the age of five, has become an illness of pandemic proportions?

To treat a condition you must first be able to correctly diagnose it. So let's spend a minute diagnosing the issue here. Fear of public speaking is correctly diagnosed as communication apprehension and is usually brought on by two factors:

- The formality of the speaking situation and

- The novelty of the speaking situation

This is usually reinforced by a bad public speaking experience which has cemented itself as a belief in your subconscious mind which has now left you unable to stand up and speak naturally in front of a group of people.

Once your mind accepts a belief it becomes self-reinforcing and your subconscious will actively seek out ways to avoid public speaking situations in order to 'protect' you – it is survival instinct at its most basic.

Formality

The formality of the experience refers to the setting (which could be a stadium, a school, a church, a boardroom or anywhere else) and the situation (job interview, sales pitch, meeting, eulogy, presentation). This fear is linked to the fear of 'not knowing what to say' and 'looking like a fool in front of others'.

In our minds there is something very different between sitting and holding a conversation with others and standing and talking to the same group, this difference is purely perception as we are essentially trying to have conversation level confidence in any situation, where you are no longer focussed on your words or your posture but purely the message.

Novelty

The experience of public speaking is only novel because you do not have experience;

this is true for every experience in your life. It was the same when you took your first steps or when you said your first word but thankfully that never stopped you from either talking or walking in later life.

I am lucky enough to have two wonderful children, the second of which, my daughter has just taken her first few steps at the time of writing this book and it amazes me how many times she falls over and hurts herself, but despite the bruises she gets back up and continues. Thankfully we all know that the first few steps will always be the hardest and as she gets more confident on her feet this will become a far less painful experience. Public speaking is exactly the same, you need to push on and realise that it is ok to fall as long as you get back up again.

Exposure therapy

The key to overcoming commination anxiety is exposure – referred to scientifically as systematic desensitisation. There are examples of how effective this is this working all around us, to illustrate I would like to walk you through two examples.

Horses often have a natural fear of cars, and why wouldn't they? They are noisy and not found in nature. If you put a horse in a field next to a major road, they will become completely calm around cars to the point where they don't even notice them anymore.

When treating phobias such as the fear of spiders, one of the most effective treatments is controlled exposure therapy, starting with a spider in a clear box and moving closer until you are comfortable and then eventually holding the spider in your hand for a period of time. Once people realise that they are not waiting for their chance to bite you they begin to recondition their minds to remove the irrational fear and can then even grow to like these fascinating creatures.

To practically apply this technique you should build up your exposure to public speaking, beginning with small, impromptu speeches and working your way up to longer presentations in front of larger audiences. Wherever possible, practice in the same location that you will preparing the speech to familiarise yourself to the location and surroundings; if you will be presenting while standing up then practice in the same way to make the 'dress rehearsal' as realistic as possible.

You can also use the below technique to accelerate your exposure therapy:

Lay down or sit somewhere you can comfortably relax and close your eyes and picture yourself in front of an audience giving a presentation, you are addressing the group in a calm and confident way. You may feel some anxiety to begin with but this will reduce with repetition.

As you feel more relaxed in this situation then repeat the exercise but slowly increase the size of the audience. You can make the setting more formal or increase the importance of the speech in your mind until it begins to feel slightly outside of your comfort zone.

This technique is useful in supporting your public speaking efforts in reducing anxiety but it will not replace exposure to real life situations. Be careful to gradually increase your mental levels of exposure and make sure before you begin that you are committed to repeating this exercise over time until you are in a relaxed state, otherwise you could increase your anxiety levels and then abandon this method which would have the effect of further reinforcing your anxiety levels.

Creating a Peak state

Reducing anxiety in itself is not sufficient to make you a good or even great public speaker. As mentioned earlier you want to aim for 'conversation level confidence' in a public setting; to achieve this you need to be operating in a "Peak state" where you are naturally confident and able to respond appropriately to the audience, the subject and anything that may come your way.

To operate in a peak state where you are at your best and able to think clearly and respond appropriately to the audience, questions, interruptions or anything else that comes your way you need to be operating at a peak state.

The way you achieve this state is through

the following:

- Increasing experience,

- Increasing knowledge, and

- Reducing anxiety

Increasing Experience: As mentioned above, you can become completely comfortable whilst standing and speaking to groups of people through practice and exposure.

Increasing knowledge: Chapters 3 and 4 will provide you with the framework and the knowledge to underpin your efforts in this area.

The combination of the increase in knowledge and exposure will naturally reduce your levels of anxiety.

Peak State: once you have the knowledge, exposure (experience) and are freed from the anxiety that would have previous hindered your public speaking efforts you will be able to be naturally confident and deliver at your best.

Remember:

You can reduce anxiety by increasing your knowledge

You can remove anxiety through repeated exposure and changing the way you think about speaking

P.E.A.K model

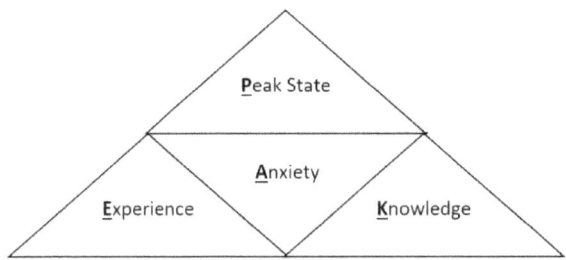

To really increase your chances of successful recall you should draw out these diagrams, adding your own notes, and mnemonics as you go until you have committed this to memory, repeat this process in one day and then again in one week to push this into your long term memory.

CHAPTER 3: CRAFTING YOUR SPEECH

We are trying to achieve one thing - Essentially we are having a private conversation in public, in order to do that you need to be able to;

- Structure thoughts logically, and

- Deliver your speech clearly

Crafting a powerful speech is an important part of public speaking and a well-defined speech will ensure that you always remain focussed and in control of your speech.

In this chapter we will touch on the first of

the three building block of public speaking:

- Memory.

- Arrangement, and

- Invention

Memory does not relate to memorising your speech word for word; rather, it relates to two things, being able to remember the key points of your speech and their order (covered under invention and arrangement below) but more transitionally to being able to recall stories and anecdotes as well as having a bank of general knowledge to rely on during your speech.

Invention relates to the creation of content, identifying what material is appropriate for your speech and your audience to support your message. Invention does not relate to the logical order of these ideas.

Arrangement is the next stage in the process of crafting your speech and relates to the logical ordering of your ideas so they have the biggest impact on your audience.

The key to crafting a compelling speech for any situation firstly relies in understanding the differences between written and spoken word. Most people will simply 'write' a good speech and then try to commit it all to memory or even read it out word for word 'on the day'.

Speeches are designed to be spoken, not simply read, we all naturally speak in a different way to our written style and we need to bear this in mind when preparing a speech.

Preparing a speech:

- Speech goals,

- Speech constraints, and

- Outlining

Speech Goals:

Speech goals are a powerful way of ensuring that your final presentation is well received and achieves your speech objectives. Your speech will usually have at least one primary speech goal with a number of supporting secondary speech goals; your primary speech goal is related to what you are hoping to achieve through your speech whilst your secondary speech goals are related to what you would like the audience to achieve from the speech which could be a change in opinion or a call to action depending on the nature of the speech. For speech goals to be effective they need to be defined.

Example:

You have been asked to deliver a key note speech at a charity fundraiser for a cancer research charity. There are hundreds of wealthy guests and you have been asked to produce a compelling speech to encourage the audience to dig deep and donate to the charity.

Your primary speech goal here could be 'To raise money for the charity' whilst your secondary speech goals could be 'To help the audience understand the recent research breakthroughs, the impact of these breakthroughs and the funding requirement to develop research trials.

Speech Constraints:

Constraints:

- Topic,

- Occasion,

- Audience

- Setting, and

- Time

Topic:

If the topic of the speech has been set for you then you will need to ensure that you present your arguments to support this.

Occasion:

The speaking occasion could bring with it a number of cultural expectations that you may need to observe in terms of content or arrangement; a wedding speech carries with it very different expectations than a eulogy, both of which will vary depending on the culture of the audience.

Audience:

Your audience constraints relate to the collective understanding of the subject area being discussed and their ability to absorb the information you present.

Setting:

The setting of the speech could vary considerably from one speech to another and could reasonably impact what you say, for example giving a speech at a primary school may dictate the use of more carefully selected words than one delivered in a sports club.

Time:

Time refers to the time allocated to the speech. You may have been asked to speak for 10 minutes or 2 hours in which case your time constraint will have a major impact on the speech content and the arguments you employ.

Types of speeches

- Impromptu speech

- Informative speech, and

- Persuasive speech

Impromptu speech

Impromptu speeches are the most common type of speaking situations that you are likely to come across in a business or academic situation. These types of speeches are often the hardest to prepare for as they come about at little or no notice but thankfully seem to be the shortest.

Informative speech

Informative speeches are designed to transfer knowledge or a message from the speaker to the audience.

Persuasive speech

Persuasive speeches are often regarded as the hardest of the three types of speech as these are designed to elicit a response from the audience, usually in the form of agreement or a decision.

Outlining

The key to writing an effective speech is to structure your ideas in a clear and logical order that supports your arguments, not writing the speech out word for word. Remember, the focus here is on public speaking and not on public reading.

The way you achieve this is by creating a speech 'outline'. This is nothing more than the main points of your speech in the order you wish to state them. If your speech were a book, then your outline would be the table of contents.

Your outline will then serve as a reminder of the main topics not the individual words that you will be conveying in your speech. This gives you the freedom to deliver your speech in a natural and conversational way rather than sounding robotic and scripted. The goal here is to create a good speech, not to create a good outline.

Sample outline: Impromptu speech

Thesis statement

Preview statement

Claim (1)

       Support (1.1)

       Support (1.2)

Claim (2)

       Support (2.1)

       Support (2.2)

Summary Statement

Conclusion

You have already come across this structure in chapter 1 of this book:

[Thesis statement] Public speaking is an important and worthwhile skill that can be learnt in less than 60 minutes. Fact.

[Preview statement] There are few born public speakers and at its most basic, as a skill it is inextricably linked to career success.

[Claim (1)] Managers at all levels are expected to be able to communicate clearly and concisely.

[Support (1.1)] Put simply, to lead effectively you must be able to communicate direction and goals effectively;

[Support (1.2)] this is even more important as you progress to the top of an organisation and becomes an expectation at board level.

[Claim (2)] There are few 'born' public speakers;

[Support (2.1)] importantly this means that there are thousands of 'polished' public speakers. If thousands of others have learned to speak effectively in public then you can too.

[Support (2.2)] With a few simple tools you will be able to master the art of creating compelling content and delivering a powerful speech.

[Summary Statement] Through the next few chapters you will learn more about this important and worthwhile skill as well as a simple framework to help you remember this for years to come.

[Conclusion] I would like to wish you the very best on your public speaking journey.

Sample outline: Informative speech

Intro
Open the speech
State the thesis statement

Preview both of the main points

    Transition to main point 1

        Support 1

        Support 2

    Transition to main point 2

        Support 1

        Support 2

Transition to conclusion

Restate thesis and main points

Conclude speech

Remember:

Constraints (TOAST)

- Topic

- Occasion

- Audience

- Setting

- Time

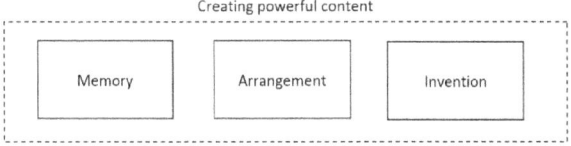

To really increase your chances of successful recall you should draw out these diagrams, adding your own notes, and mnemonics as you go until you have committed this to memory, repeat this process in one day and then again in one week to push this into your long term memory.

CHAPTER 4: DOING IT IN STYLE

I once attended a public speaking group and there were a number of new members present all of whom were told that at some point during the meeting that they would be expected to stand up and give a short, two minute speech on a subject of their choosing. As the evening progressed the new members were asked to speak one at a time until they all had their moment in the spotlight, the quality ranged from average to poor, so much so that many in the this category had to sit down half way through their speech due to nerves.

One lady, who did not speak English as her first language stood up and immediately her mind went blank. Thirty long painful seconds passed as she couldn't find any words to fill the silence. Rather than sit down like many of her peers she just started posing, she laughed and then held a pose like she was in a photo shoot, a few of the audience laughed, most were puzzled. She then continued this farce until the whole audience was roaring with laughter. Despite not saying a single word during the entire two minutes she ended up winning the impromptu speech category that evening due to her style and her delivery.

This chapter covers the final two building blocks;

- Delivery

- Style

Delivery

To support these final two building blocks I have developed a framework that will walk you through some of the focus areas that I refer to as the 6 P's' of presence;

- Projection

- Pace

- Pitch

- Personalisation

- Persuasion

- Practice

Projection

Projection refers to the qualities of your

voice including the volume and direction. You need to ensure that your audience can clearly hear you which is much more than simply speaking loudly.

The most important element of projection is without a doubt diaphragmatic breathing, which will result in deeper breaths which will supply more oxygen to your brain and your muscles. You can easily determine if you are breathing correctly (using your diaphragm) by placing your hand on your stomach when you breath, you should feel your stomach move but not your shoulders. This is how babies breathe naturally but as we grow we develop bad habits in later life. This may take some practice until it feels natural but it is an easy and important change to make.

Projection is about speaking with the power and confidence that is appropriate to your speech setting and your material.

Pace

When presenting to an audience, you need to ensure that your speaking rate (pace) is appropriate to the group, speaking too fast will lose the audience and reduce comprehension of the subject matter, too slow will lose the audience's interest.

The average speaking rate is between 125 to 175 words per minute and whilst there is no 'correct' rate of speech, your focus should be on ensuring that your rate is varied and appropriate to your audience and your material.

Different speeds portray different messages to your audience, to convey excitement, speak more rapidly, just as you would in everyday life. When you discuss important points, keep your pace slow and deliberate. As a general rule speaking slowly adds credibility, it is hard to convey excitement at this pace; if it sounds slow in your head, it is probably about right.

Benefits of speaking slowly:

- Portrays confidence

- Gives the audience a chance to absorb the information

- Gives you as the speaker time to think

- Appears deliberate

Pausing & Silence

Silence is inherently uncomfortable for some and feels particularly uncomfortable when you are in a public "speaking" scenario, after all aren't your supposed to be speaking? The use of silence can be a powerful addition to your speaking toolkit and can add emphasis in a way that words may be unable to convey, pausing is the speech equivalent of punctuation and it is essential to the successful delivery of your presentation.

Silence is essentially an exaggerated pause and can be used effectively in a number of scenarios such as following a question you have posed to the audience, or a key point that you want the audience to think about before you move onto the next point.

Pitch

Pitch relates to how high or low your voice is, it is generally accepted that speaking at the same tone for long periods of time will almost certainly lose your audience. When speaking you should be aiming for vocal variety, but more specifically 'natural variety'. You do not want to assume a tone that is uncomfortable to maintain or that does not feel natural as the audience will immediately pick up on this.

We are aiming for conversation level variety. When you express excitement and enthusiasm in a conversation it is often expressed at a higher pitch compared to something more personal like a painful memory which might be lower and more sombre.

Practice tonal variety in your everyday speech to naturally incorporate this into your public speaking.

Personalisation

Throughout this book I have referred to achieving 'conversation level confidence' this essentially refers to all of the positive attributes that you bring to everyday speaking. You will unconsciously have natural tonal variation, projection and pitch that you have developed over a lifetime so do not make the mistake of copying somebody else's speaking style. By all means, use roles models to help you develop your own speaking persona, but ensure that you make their best characteristics your own.

When presenting to an audience try to be as natural as possible, remember, we are trying to achieve conversation level confidence in a public setting; the ability to flow between one topic and another, the ability to respond to questions or issues as they arise throughout your presentation in the same way you do in everyday life.

Filler phrases

Filler words and phrases like "erm" or "like" are pervasive in speaking, if you use filler words in your everyday conversation then continue to use them in your speech. Focussing too much in this area will only add to any communication anxiety, the trick here is that if they really bothers you then work on removing them in your everyday life, that way this will naturally pull through in your public speaking.

Here are a few simple tips for improving your public speaking outside of a presentation:

- Work on improving your everyday speech outside of a public speaking situation

- Improve your vocabulary (invest in a thesaurus)

- Work on removing filler words from your every speech

Using gestures

Gestures provide additional visual stimuli

for your audience and are favourable to the alternative of standing completely still whilst you deliver your speech. Try to incorporate natural gestures and gradually expand your range when you feel comfortable. Imagine a 'gesture box' as seen in the illustration below, wherever possible, do not extend your gestures outside of this area.

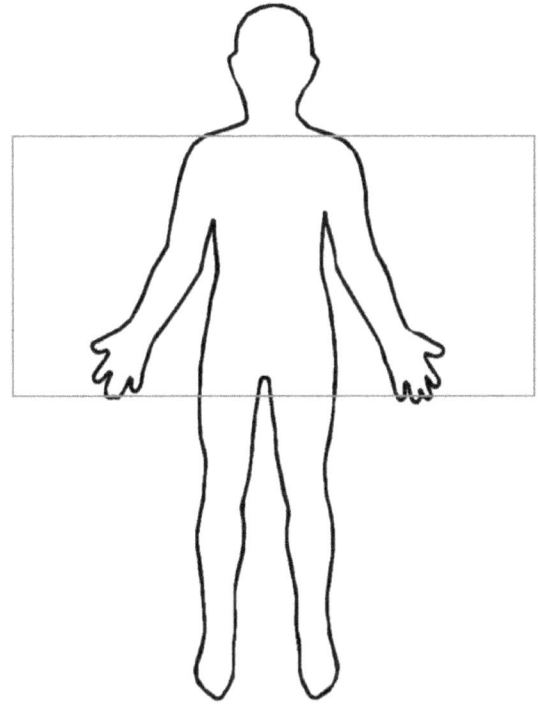

If you do not naturally gesture when presenting then you can mimic gestures from other speakers who you admire, but be careful not to simply copy them. Practice them, adapt them and make them your own.

Persuasion

Persuasion is the selection of words and phrases that will evoke a response in your audience; this can be one of the hardest elements of speaking to master. You are essentially asking the audience for a change from the status quo; this could be a change of mind set, a change of behaviours, or parting with money.

The basis of the persuasion, your ideas, would be covered under the 'invention' building block and would be detailed in your speech outline, so this section does not deal with your basic argument, purely the selection of words used to convey the message in the most effective and powerful way to your audience.

The "SEEM" model:

- Say it

- Explain it

- Evidence it

- MOVE ON!

Say it: Tell the audience what your supporting evidence is in simple terms as a preview of the next chunk of your material.

Explain it: Provide clear information on how this point relates and supports your claim.

Evidence it: Tell the audience why this is true.

Move on: Once you have made your point

move on. Think of it like a tradesman hammering in a nail. Once you have hammered the nail home, any further hammering will simply damage the area.

Practice

Professional speakers will practice their speech outline using a method called chunking. They will repeat this process a minimum of 30 times before they present to their audience.

Remember the goals is to deliver a clear and concise speech that doesn't 'look' rehearsed.

Chunking

Chunking is the process of practising 'chunks' of your presentation based on your outline i.e. introduction / conclusion or specific stories, illustrations or claims.

Chunking is a powerful way of memorising the important points of your speech including transitions between points, without trying to memorise your speech word for word.

Keep the practise environment as close to the live environment as possible, if you will be standing then stand

Style

Style is the fifth and final building block of successful public speaking. There are a number of stylistics devices that have been around for thousands of years, having stood the test of time. Below is a summary of the key techniques you should familiarise yourself with simplified to help you recall them during your speech when you'll need them the most. I have distilled them in to the "6 A's of Style":

- Alliteration

- Asynden

- Anaphora

- Antithesis

- Antimetabole

- Apositio

You will no doubt recognise many of the below examples of stylistic devices, in many cases more than one stylistic device is at work, where this is the case I have included the same reference again to demonstrate each principle at work.

Alliteration

Alliteration is the use of words that begin with the same consonants which can be compared to Assonance, the use of words that begin with the same vowels. Alliteration has been used widely to great effect and has been included in many political speeches around the world. It assists in distilling ideas into a form that people can relate to and remember.

"...and that government of the People, by the People, for the People shall not Perish from the earth".

Abraham Lincoln, Gettysburg Address

Asyndeton

Asyndeton is the omission of naturally

occurring conjunctions. Winston Churchill's address, "We shall fight on the beaches" is a prime example of the use of Asyndeton.

"We shall go on to the end, we shall fight in France, we shall fight on the seas and oceans, we shall fight with growing confidence and growing strength in the air, we shall defend our Island, whatever the cost may be, we shall fight on the beaches, we shall fight on the landing grounds, we shall fight in the fields and in the streets, we shall fight in the hills; we shall never surrender. . ."

Winston Churchill, "We shall fight on the beaches" speech

Note also: Polysyndeton, inserting

excessive use of conjunctions. The below example is a variation of the famous Winston Churchill speech to demonstrate how this could have looked had Polysyndeton been chosen as the stylistic device:

We shall go on to the end <u>and</u> we shall fight in France <u>and</u> we shall fight on the seas and oceans <u>and</u> we shall fight with growing confidence and growing strength in the air <u>and</u> we shall defend our Island <u>and</u> whatever the cost may be <u>and</u> we shall fight on the beaches <u>and</u> we shall fight on the landing ground <u>and</u>, we shall fight in the fields and in the streets <u>and</u> we shall fight in the hills <u>and</u> we shall never surrender. . .

Winston Churchill, "We shall fight on the beaches" speech [Adapted]

Anaphora

Anaphora is the repetition of the first word or set of words at the beginning of a sentence or phrase (this should be the key phrase for it to be successful)

"We shall go on to the end, we shall fight in France, we shall fight on the seas and oceans, we shall fight with growing confidence and growing strength in the air, we shall defend our Island, whatever the cost may be, we shall fight on the beaches, we shall fight on the landing grounds, we shall fight in the fields and in the streets, we shall fight in the hills; we shall never surrender. . ."

Note also: Epistrophe, the repetition of a word or phrase at the end of every clause.

"...and that government of <u>the people</u>, by <u>the people</u>, for <u>the people</u> shall not perish from the earth".

Abraham Lincoln, Gettysburg Address

Note also: Symploce, the repetition or a word or phrase at the beginning and the end of a sentence.

Anadiplosis

Anadiplosis is the repetition of the last word of a preceding clause. Essentially, the word is used at the end of a sentence and then used again at the beginning of the next sentence

"Watch your 'thoughts, for they will become actions. Watch your actions, for they'll become... habits. Watch your habits for they will forge your character. Watch your character, for it will make your destiny." Margaret Thatcher in the motion picture The Iron Lady.

DK the only thing to fear, is fear itself

Antithesis

Antithesis is where two opposites are introduced in the same sentence, for contrasting effect:

"Ask not what your country can do for you, ask what you can do for your country."

John F. Kennedy, Inaugural Address, 1961

Note also: Antimetabole, the repetition of words in successive clauses, but in transposed order i.e. clauses 1-2-2-1; the above is an example of both antithesis and antimetabole at work.

The difference between Antithesis and Antimetabole, is that antithesis contrasts opposing ideas whereas Antimetabole contrasts the use of words.

Appositio

Appositio is the elaboration and variation of a word in a sentence.

A man faithful in friendship, prudent in counsels, virtuous in conversation, gentle in communication, learned in all liberal sciences, eloquent in utterance, comely in gesture, an enemy to naughtiness, and a lover of all virtue and godliness.

JFK eulogy (need reference)

Summary:

- Don't copy other people's speaking style directly…be yourself.

- Focus NOT on yourself, but focus on really helping your audience understand.

- Work on improving your everyday speech outside of a public speaking situations and this will naturally improve your public speaking ability.

- Improve your vocabulary in your every day life

- Work on removing filler words from your

every speech

- Analyse others gestures and personalise them, make them your own

- Use stylistic devices to add power to your presentation

Remember:

The two building blocks covered in this section were:

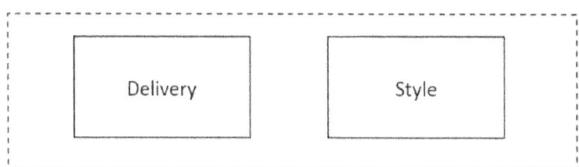

These can be further broken down into the "6 P's of Delivery" and the "6 A's of Style":

Delivery	Style
Projection	Alliteration
Pace	Asynden
Pitch	Anaphora
Personalisation	Antithesis
Persuasion	Antimetabole
Practice	Apositio

CHAPTER 5: PUSHING THE PANIC BUTTON

So you have a speech and you feel less than prepared. Follow the tips below to ensure you can perform at your best in the time available

Preparation

1. Know your outline: Pick a topic you are interested in. Know more about it than you include in your speech. Use personal stories and conversational language – that way you won't easily forget what to say.

2. Practice: Practice as many times running

all the way through as you are able to fit into the time you have available, make changes to your outline to any parts that you feel need amending and repeat.

Communication anxiety

Last minute nerves are a natural part of public speaking, repeated exposure will continually reduce any anxiety you feel before a speech, the important thing is to acknowledge it and then move on.

3. Visualize yourself giving your speech. Picture a slightly more confident version of you, standing in front of your audience, speaking clearly and confidently.

4. Ask yourself "what are my speech goals". Concentrate on the audience and meeting

these goals, remember your primary speech goals should always be focussed on the audience and never on yourself. Focus on helping your audience understand your message.

Delivery

5. Speak slowly - if it sounds slow in your head, it's probably about right.

6. Speak naturally - don't try to become a good public speaker, just try to speak like a normal person while in public.

Many people end a presentation with the phrase "Any Questions?"; do not make this mistake, this is a transition and not a conclusion and a close as weak as this will at best detract from your message and all of your hard work.

Handling questions

For some speakers, being asked a difficult question whilst addressing an audience is a major source of communication anxiety (subordinate fear). Thankfully, there are a few simple steps you can follow that can make handling questions during or after your speech a more structured experience as a speaker.

7. State your 'rules of engagement'.

Before you enter into the body of your speech, state the rules of engagement to your audience; if you plan to have a questions and answers section in your presentation then state this at the outset of your speech, and be sure to let the audience know when it is appropriate, otherwise you may well be bombarded with questions throughout your presentation.

If you do not want to take questions then do not be afraid to say this this at the outset. A simple phrase like "I will not be taking any questions today but would be more than happy to follow up any questions you may have individually over the next few days".

1. Repeat the question for the group. Re-state the questions to confirm understanding if the question is ambiguous or complex. This will buy time to think of an answer as well as confirming that you have fully understood the question.

2. If you cannot answer the question on the

spot then I would suggest that you explain why the question is actually more complex than it seems and for that reason you would be happy to discuss individually with them after

3. Finally, if you have a really persistent questioner who simply will not leave you alone then re-state that you will answer that question "offline" and ask them to speak to you as soon as you finish.

Remember, it is your presentation and you are in control.

CHAPTER 6: PUTTING IT ALL TOGETHER

You now have everything you need to create and deliver a professional and compelling presentation, we just need to put it all together into a single model that you can refer back to in the future as you develop your public speaking abilities.

1. Identify your speech goals, what are you trying to teach your audience? How are you trying to persuade them? What are the benefits of your speech to them? These will always be focussed on the needs of your audience.

2. Identify your speech constraints using thee TOAST model. Ensure that the speech is appropriate for the speaking situation.

3. Prepare an outline. Use bullet points to capture key concepts, breaking your speech down into memorable chunks.

4. Review your outline incorporating the five building blocks to ensure that all of the essential elements of a good speech have been included.

- Is the speech memorable (broken down into chunks)?

- Is the arrangement appropriate for your speech constraints?

- Are you points well-structured and logical

(Invention)?

- Is the speech written is a way that will allow you to delivery it in a natural way that you are comfortable with?

- Have you included the use of one or more stylistic devices to add emphasis around your key points?

5. Practice your speech all the way through and change as necessary

6. Focus on your delivery and give the best speech you can, speak slowly, speak clearly.

7. Live and Learn – the best way to truly master public speaking is to practice speaking in front of audiences. Seek out opportunities to practice your new found skills, each presentation you deliver will

provide you with feedback to further tailor your approach and will bring you one step closer to public speaking mastery.

To help you remember the 60 Minute Public Speaking framework I have devised the analogy of a house. The foundations being preparation, the house consisting of the '5 building blocks of public speaking' and the roof made up of the peak state model. To really increase your chances of successful recall you should draw out these diagrams, adding your own notes, and mnemonics as you go until you have committed this to memory, repeat this process in one day and then again in one week to push this into your long term memory.

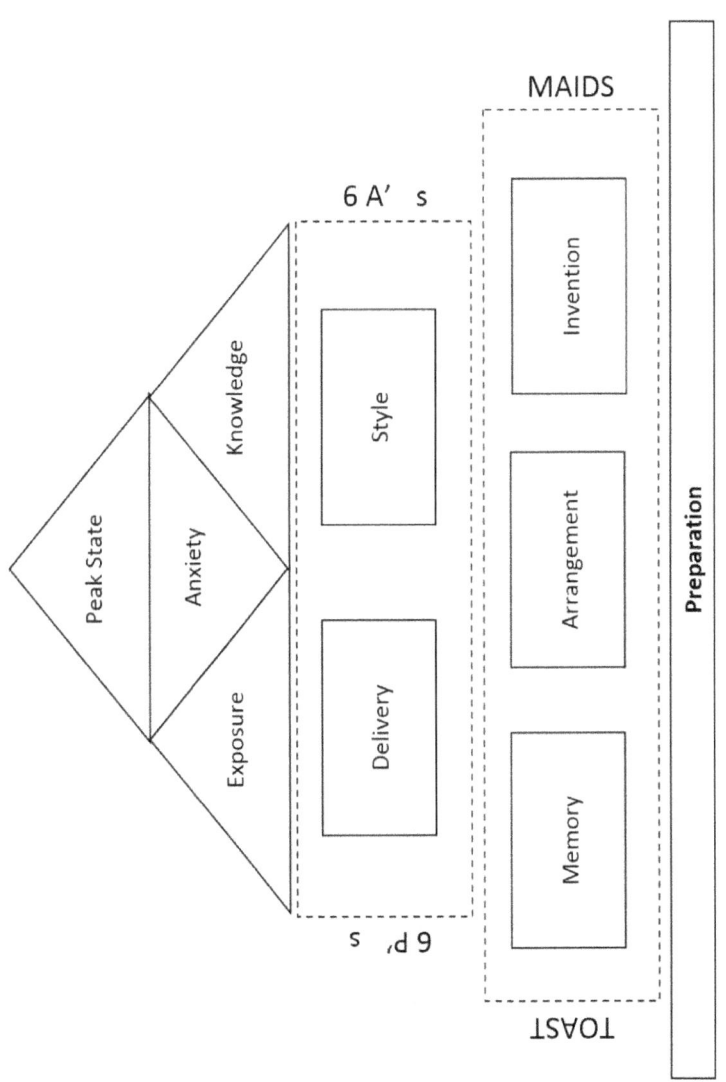

GLOSSARY

Arrangement

The process of arranging and organizing your arguments for maximum impact.

Alliteration

The use of words that begin with the same continents

Anadiplosis

Anadiplosis is the repetition of the last word of a preceding clause

Anaphora

Anaphora is the repetition of the first word or set of words at the beginning of a sentence or phrase

Antimetabole

Antimetabole is a stylistic device which contrasts the use of words

Antithesis

Antithesis is a stylistic device which contrasts opposing ideas

Apositio

Apositio is a stylistic device where a single word of phrase is elaborated and varied

Assertion (claim)

Assertion (claim)

Assonance

The use of words that begin with the same vowels

Asynden

The omission of naturally occurring conjunctions

Audience

This refers to the recipients of your speech

Claim

See assertion

Conclusion

Conclusions are a structure ending to your speech in which you summarise your key points

Constraints

Constraints are any external restrictions placed on you or your speech which may include topic or time

Delivery

The process of practicing how you deliver your speech using gestures, pronunciation, and tone of voice.

Epistrophe

The repetition of a word or phrase at the end of every clause.

Evidence

Your supporting argument

Ice Breaker

Ice Breakers are short stories or group exercises designed to 'break the ice' and break down barriers between the speaker and the audience or amongst the audience themselves.

Invention

The process of developing and refining your arguments.

Impromptu

Impromptu refers to having little or no preparation prior to speaking

Memory

The process of learning and memorizing your speech so you can deliver it without the use of notes.

Occasion

Occasion refers to the event at which you are speaking (wedding, funeral, sales pitch)

Outline

A bullet pointed summary of the presentation which captures the main points of your speech and their order

Outlining

The process of creating a speech outline

Pace

Pace refers to the speed of your speech, it is often measured in the number of spoken words per minute (wpm)

Persuasion

The act of changing the minds of your audience through your argument and its supporting evidence

Pitch

The tone of your voice

Polysyndeton

The excessive use of conjunctions

Rhetoric

Rhetoric is the 'art of persuasion', which is considered one of the definitions of public speaking

Setting

Setting refers to the surroundings of where you will deliver your speech which could include a stage in a grand hall, a podium, a lectern or a board room

Style

The process of determining how you present your arguments using figures of speech and other rhetorical techniques

Summary

A brief recap of the presentation in which you restate the main points

Support

Subordinate statement directly linked to your claims designed to further or illustrate your argument

Symploce

The repetition of a word or phrase at both the beginning and the end of every clause

Thesis

Thesis is the basis of your argument in your presentation. It is the point of view of the speaker in which the speech is founded

Time

The time allocated for the speech

Topic

Subject area of your speech

PUBLIC SEAKING RESOURCES

Speaking clubs

Powertalk International

https://www.powertalkinternational.com/

Speaking Circles

http://www.speakingcircles.com/

Toastmasters International

http://www.toastmasters.org/

Association of Speakers Clubs

http://www.the-asc.org.uk/

Ice breakers

Over 600 Icebreakers & Games [Kindle Edition] (Jennifer carter)

Ice Breakers! How to Get Any Prospect to Beg You for a Presentation (Tom Schreiter)

Jokes and humour

After Dinner Laughs: Jokes and Funny Stories for Speechmakers (Hugh Morrison)

The Serious Guide to Joke Writing: How to Say Something Funny about Anything (Sally Holloway)

Thought field therapy

https://www.youtube.com/watch?v=g8nF 8rdDxGs (YouTube)

ABOUT THE AUTHOR

Stewart is an award winning Chartered Manager, qualified Accountant and Project Manager with a number of year's professional experience delivering business change and managing complex projects within the Financial Services industry in multi-national organisations and listed PLCs.

Also by this Author

60 Minute: Scrum

Scrum is a project management approach based on Agile principles that allows organisations and individuals to deliver the highest possible value in the shortest possible time. This framework has often been met with adversity as it is a departure to traditional methods, but has stood the test of time and has demonstrated through countless organisations that they are able to deliver more with less.

ISBN: 9781301073139

Available on: Kindle. iBooks, Audible, Nook and other popular e-readers.

60 Minute: Exam Success

60 Minute Exam Success provides an easy to follow framework that greatly increase your chances of success in your upcoming exam. The book walks you through a number of approaches to amplify our own revision efforts, giving you the best chances of exam success in the minimum amount of time. This book has been engineered to be read in less than an hour, but its benefits will last you a lifetime.

ISBN: 9781311694133

Available on: Kindle. iBooks, Audible, Barnes & Noble, Nook and other popular e-readers.